How To Get Money for Small Business Start Up

How to Get Massive Money from Crowdfunding, Government Grants and Government Loans

By Ramsey Colwell

DEDICATION

This book is dedicated to my son's
Christian and Matthew.
A blessing from God and the joy of my life.

ACKNOWLEDGMENTS

I WOULD LIKE TO ACKNOWLEDGE ALL THE HARD WORK OF THE MEN AND WOMEN OF THE UNITED STATES MILITARY, WHO RISK THEIR LIVES ON A DAILY BASIS, TO MAKE THE WORLD A SAFER PLACE.

Disclaimer

This book was written as a guide to starting a business. As with any other high yielding action, starting a business has a certain degree of risk. This book is not meant to take the place of accounting, legal, financial or other professional advice. If advice is needed in any of these fields, you are advised to seek the services of a professional.

While the author has attempted to make the information in this book as accurate as possible, no guarantee is given as to the accuracy or currency of any individual item. Laws and procedures related to business are constantly changing.

Therefore, in no event shall Brian Mahoney or MahoneyProducts Publishers be liable for any special indirect, or consequential damages or any damages whatsoever in connection with the use of the information herein provided.

Table of Contents

Chapter 1

How Do I Start a Small Business

There are over thirty million home-based businesses in the United States alone.

Many people dream of the independence and financial reward of having a home business. Unfortunately they let analysis paralysis stop them from taking action. This chapter is designed to give you a road map to get started. The most difficult step in any journey is the first step.

Anthony Robbins created a program called Personal Power. I studied the program a long time ago, and today I would summarize it, by saying you must figure out a way to motivate yourself to take massive action without fear of failure.

2 Timothy 1:7 King James Version

"For God hath not given us the spirit of fear; but of power, and of love, and of a sound mind."

STEP #1 MAKE AN OFFICE IN YOUR HOUSE

If you are serious about making money, then redo the man cave or the woman's cave and make a place for you to do business, uninterupted.

STEP #2 BUDGET OUT TIME FOR YOUR BUSINESS

If you already have a job, or if you have children, then they can take up a great deal of your time. Not to mention well meaning friends who use the phone to become time theives. Budget time for your business and stick to it.

STEP #3 DECIDE ON THE TYPE OF BUSINESS

You don't have to be rigid, but begin with the end in mine. You can become more flexible as you gain experience.

STEP #4 LEGAL FORM FOR YOUR BUSINESS

The three basic legal forms are sole proprietorship, partnership, and corporation. Each one has it's advantages. Go to www.Sba.gov and learn about each and make a decision.

STEP #5 PICK A BUSINESS NAME AND REGISTER IT

One of the safest ways to pick a business name is to use your own name. By using your own name you don't have to worry about copy right violations.

However, always check with an Attorney or the proper legal authority when dealing with legal matters.

STEP #6 WRITE A BUSINESS PLAN

This would seem like a no brainer. No matter what you are trying to accomplish you should have a blueprint. You should have a business plan. In the NFL about seven headcoaches get fired every season. So in a very competetive business, a man with no head coaching experience got hired by the NFL's Philadelphia Eagles. His name was Andy Reid. Andy Reid would later become the most successful coach in the team's history. One of the reasons the owner hired him, was because he had a business plan the size of a telephone book. Your business plan does not need to be nearly that big, but if you plan for as much as possible, you are less likely to get rattled when things don't go as planned.

STEP #7 PROPER LICENSES & PERMITS

Go to city hall and find out what you need to do, to start a home business.

STEP #8 PUT UP A WEB SITE, SELECT BUSINESS CARDS, STATIONERY, BROCHURES

This is one of the least expensive ways to not only start your business but to promote and network your business.

STEP #9 OPEN A BUSINESS CHECKING ACCOUNT

Having a separate business account makes it much easier to keep track of profit and expenses. This will come in handy, whether you decide to do your own taxes or hire out an professional.

STEP #10 TAKE SOME SORT OF ACTION TODAY

This is not meant to be a comprehensive plan to start a business. It is meant to point you in the right direction to get started. You can go to the Small Business Administration for many free resources for starting your business. They even have a program(SCORE) that will give you access to many retired professionals who will advise you for free! Their web site: **www.score.org**

Chapter 2

Colossal Cash

from

Crowd Funding

Crowd Funding Crowd Sourcing

In 2015 over $34 billion dollars was raised by crowdfunding. Crowdfunding and Crowdsourcing roots began in 2005 and they help to finance or fund projects by raising money from a large number of people, usually by using the internet.

This type of fundraising or venture capital usually has 3 components. The individual or organization with a project that needs funding, groups of people who donate to the project, and a organization sets up a structure or rules to put the two together.

These websites do charge fees. The standard fee for success is about %5. If your goal is not met there is also a fee.

Below is a list of the top Crowdfunding websites according to myself and Entrepreneur Magazine Contributor Sally Outlaw.

Crowd Funding Crowd Sourcing

https://www.indiegogo.com/

Started as a platform for getting movies made, now helps to raise funds for any cause.

http://rockethub.com/

Started as a platform for the arts, now it helps to raise funds for business, science, social projects and education.

http://peerbackers.com/

Peerbackers focuses on raising funds for business, entrepreneurs and innovators.

https://www.kickstarter.com/

The most popular and well know n of all the crowdfunding websites. Kickstarter focuses on film, music, technology, gaming, design and the creative arts. Kickstarter only accepts projects from the United States, Canada and the United Kingdom.

Crowd Funding Crowd Sourcing

Group Growvc

http://group.growvc.com/

This website is for business and technology innovation.

https://microventures.com/

Get access to angel investors. This website is for business startups.

https://angel.co/

Another website for business startups.

https://circleup.com/

Circle up is for innovative consumer companies.

https://www.patreon.com/

If you start a YouTube Channel (highly recommended) you will hear about this website frequently. This website is for creative content people.

Crowd Funding Crowd Sourcing

https://www.crowdrise.com/

"Raise money for any cause that inspires you."
The Landing page slogan speaks for itself. #1
fundraising website for personal causes.

https://www.gofundme.com/

This fundraising website allows for business, charity
education, emergencies, sports, medical, memorials,
animals, faith, family, newlyweds etc...

https://www.youcaring.com/

The leader in free fundraising. Over $400 million
raised.

https://fundrazr.com/

FundRazr is an award-winning online fundraising
platform that has helped thousands of people and
organizations raise money
for causes they care about.

Chapter 3

How to Apply for a Grant to Start a Small Business

Goldmine of Government Grants

Government grants. Many people either don't believe government grants exist or they don't think they would ever be able to get government grant money.

First lets make one thing clear. Government grant money is **YOUR MONEY**. Government money comes from taxes paid by residents of this country. Depending on what state you live in, you are paying taxes on almost everything....Property tax for your house. Property tax on your car. Taxes on the things you purchase in the mall, or at the gas station. Taxes on your gasoline, the food you buy etc.

So get yourself in the frame of mind that you are not a charity case or too proud to ask for help, because billionaire companies like GM, Big Banks and most of Corporate America is not hesitating to get their share of **YOUR MONEY**!

There are over two thousand three hundred (2,300) Federal Government Assistance Programs. Some are loans but many are formula grants and project grants. To see all of the programs available go to:

https://beta.sam.gov/help/assistance-listing

WRITING A GRANT PROPOSAL

The Basic Components of a Proposal

There are eight basic components to creating a solid proposal package:

1. The proposal summary;

2. Introduction of organization;

3. The problem statement   (or needs assessment)

4. Project objectives;

5. Project methods or design;

6. Project evaluation;

7. Future funding; and

8. The project budget.

WRITING A GRANT PROPOSAL

The Proposal Summary

The Proposal Summary is an outline of the project goals and objectives. Keep the Proposal Summary short and to the point. No more that 2 or 3 paragraphs. Put it at the beginning of the proposal.

Introduction

The Introduction portion of your grant proposal presents you and your business as a credible applicant and organization.

Highlight the accomplishments of your organization from all sources: newspaper or online articles etc. Include a biography of key members and leaders. State the goals and philosophy of the company.

The Problem Statement

The problem statement makes clear the problem you are going to solve(maybe reduce homelessness). Make sure to use facts. State who and how those affected will benefit from solving the problem. State the exact manner in how you will solve the problem.

WRITING A GRANT PROPOSAL

Project Objectives

The Project Objectives section of your grant proposal focuses on the Goals and Desired outcome.

Make sure to indentify all objectives and how you are going to reach these objectives. The more statistics you can find to support your objectives the better. Make sure to put in realistic objectives. You may be judged on how well you accomplish what you said you intended to do.

Program Methods and Design

The program methods and design section of your grant proposal is a detailed plan of action.

What resources are going to be used.

What staff is going to be needed.

System development.

Create a Flow Chart of project features.

Explain what will be achieved.

Try to produce evidence of what will be achieved.

Make a diagram of program design.

WRITING A GRANT PROPOSAL

Evaluation

There is product evaluation and process evaluation. The product evaluation deals with the result that relate to the project and how well the project has met it's objectives.

The process evaluation deals with how the project was conducted, how did it line up with the original stated plan and the overall effectiveness of the different aspects of the plan.

Evaluations can start at anytime during the project or at the project's conclusion. It is advised to submit a evaluation design at the start of a project.

It looks better if you have collected convincing data before and during the program.

If evaluation design is not presented at the beginning that might encourage a critical review of the program design.

Future Funding

The Future Funding part of the grant proposal should have long term project planning past the grant period.

WRITING A GRANT PROPOSAL

Budget

Utilities, rental equipment, staffing, salary, food, transportation, phone bills and insurance are just some of the things to include in the budget.

A well constructed budget accounts for every penny.

For a complete guide for government grants google

catalog of federal domestic assistance. You can download a complete PDF version of the catalog.

Other sources of Government Funding

You can get General Small Business loans from the government. Go to the Small Business Administratio for more information.

SBA Microloan Program

The Microloan program provides loans of up to $50,000 with the average loan being $13,000.

https://www.sba.gov/

Here are a Few Current Commercial Real Estate

Grant/Loan Programs

Program Number: 10.415

Program Name: Rural Rental Housing Loans

Department: Department of Agriculture

Assistance: Grants - Direct Loans

Program Number: 10.438

Program Name: Section 538 Rural Rental

Department: Department of Agriculture

Assistance: Guaranteed Loans

Program Number: 14.191

Program Name: Multifamily Housing

Department: HUD

Assistance: Project Grants

A Few Current Commercial Real Estate Grant/Loan Programs

Program Number: 14.314

Program Name: Assisted Living Conversion

Department: HUD

Assistance: Project Grants

Program Number: 14.326

Program Name: Rental Assistance 811

Department: HUD

Assistance: Project Grants

Program Number: 14.329

Program Name: HUD Multifamily PSF Pilot

Department: HUD

Assistance: Direct Payments for Specified Use

WRITING A GRANT PROPOSAL

Recently billionaire Elon Musk was awarded 4.9 billion dollars in government subsidies. If you are hesitant to pursue government assistance, let that sink in. A billionaire who pays little in taxes was given billions of your tax dollars.

Government grants are real. Like anything else worthwhile, there is effort and qualifications that must be met to obtain them.

Chapter 4

How to Apply for a Small Business Startup Loan

$5 Million Dollars to Fund Your Business

Loans guaranteed by the Small Business Administration can be as little as $500 to as big as $5 Million Dollars!

The money can be used for a variety of business needs, including the purchase of long-term fixed assets and for operating expenses. Some loan programs do have restrictions on how the loan money can be used, so you will have to check with a Small Business Administration approved lender when looking for a loan. The lender can match you with the correct loan for your business needs.

Working Capital

Like seasonal financing, export loans, revolving credit, and refinanced business debt.

Fixed Assets

Like office equipment, property, tools, machinery, business equipment, construction, and remodeling.

$5 Million Dollars to Fund Your Business

Eligibility requirements

Lenders and loan programs have distinctive eligibility guide lines. Basically, eligibility is related to what a business does to receive its funding, the character of its ownership, and location of the businesses operation. Usually, businesses must meet size standards.

What is a small business size standard?

A size standard, under most circumstances is stated in number of employees or average yearly receipts, and represents the biggest size that a business (including its subsidiaries and affiliates) may be to remain classified as a small business for Small Business Administration and government contracting programs. The definition of "small" can be different in different industries.

How to calculate your small business size

Size standards are mostly based on the average annual receipts or the average number of employees.

$5 Million Dollars to Fund Your Business

Eligibility requirements

You must be able to repay the loan. You must have credible business objective. Individuals with bad credit may still qualify for business startup money. Lenders will give you a list of the lending guide lines and requirements for your loan. Here are a few more.

Be a for-profit business

The business is properly registered and performs as legal business.

Do business in the U.S.

The business is physically located and operates in th United States and or its territories.

You Have invested equity

You the business owner has invested your own time or finances into the business.

$5 Million Dollars to Fund Your Business

Eligibility requirements

Exhaust financing options

The business cannot get money from any other financial lender.

Loans for exporters

Most United States banks view loans for exporters as risky. This can make it more difficult for you to get loans for things like day-to-day operations, advance orders with suppliers, and debt refinancing. That's why the Small Business Administration came up with programs to make it easier for United States small businesses to get loans for an export business.

To learn how the SBA can help you get an export loan, contact your local Small Business Administration International Trade Finance Specialist or the Small Business Administration's Office of International Trade.

https://www.sba.gov/funding-programs/loans

Chapter 5
YouTube
Video
Marketing

YouTube Video Marketing Overview

Million Dollar Video Marketing

When you read the title of this book you may have thought the term "Million Dollar" was hyperbole. However the beauty of video marketing is that it can be done for free, and that there really are several people who make millions of dollars just on their YouTube video's alone. Meaning that they allow ads to be placed on them and they get paid a portion of what google gets from businesses that runs the ads.

Since they are only getting a portion of what is being paid, that means if they make a million dollars, the video's actually produced multi-millions of dollars in ad revenue.

Here are a list of YouTube Millionaires as reported by Forbes magazine in the 20 December 2016 issue.

Youtube name/channel	2016 Income
1. Pewdiepie	$15 Million

Makes video's of himself playing video games and making crude comments on girls dancing.

2. Atwood	$8 Million

YouTube Video Marketing Overview

Promotes products and tours with other Youtubers.

3. Lilly Singh $7.5 Million

Makes comedy skits mostly featuring herself talking about her parents and relationship issues.

YouTube name/channel	2016 Income
4. Smosh	$7 Million

Comedy Duo.

5. Rosanna Pasino Nerdie Nummies $6 Million

Baking show

6. Markipler $5.5 Million

Comments on Video Games.

7. German Garmendia $5.5 Million

Got a publishing deal from his YouTube channel

8. Miranda Sings $5 Million

Comedian

YouTube Video Marketing Overview

9. Collen Ballinger $5 Million

Comedian

10. Tyler Oakley $5 Million

Makes a diary. LGBT Activist

And these are just some the the top earners. There are many more making $50,000 a month talking about movies, how to put on make up or video taping a day at an amusement park.

A Few Keys to Video Marketing Success

1. Commitment

While many of the top YouTubers are funny, they take their business seriously. One of the first things you have to understand is that there is commitment needed to be successful on YouTube.

Many of the successful YouTubers put up video's daily! One such YouTuber is Grace Randolph (Beyond the Trailer). Grace comments on movie news and movie trailers. She typically uploads 3 video's a day.

YouTube Video Marketing Overview

2. Research

Just putting up a video will not guarantee views. You have to put in research for every video. Research if the topic is popular or trending. Research what keywords you should use in your video. Research the success of other video's. Skip the research, skip the success.

3. Popularity

There are certain topics on YouTube that are extremely popular. Star Wars, Disney, Scantily clad women, video games, comedy. Know the level of your topics popularity and try to use keyword planning to max out the highest possible level. Some educational material is extremely valuable, but not popular.

ZERO COST MARKETING OVERVIEW

This is a zero cost online marketing plan for any business, cause or idea you wish to promote. This plan will show you step by step how to use online marketing featuring YouTube and Article Marketing to get free advertising for this or any product. In addition, this report will show you how to use this zero cost marketing plan to create a passive income stream.

YouTube Video Marketing Overview

A Few Key Definitions

YouTube is a video-sharing website headquartered in San Bruno, California, United States. The service was created by three former PayPal employee in February 2005. In November 2006, it was bought by Google for 1.65 Billion dollars. According to the Huffington Post, YouTube has 1 billion active users each month. Or nearly one out of every two people on the internet.

AdSense (Google AdSense) is an advertising placement service by Google. The program is designed for website publishers who want to display targeted text, video or image advertisement on website pages and earn money when the site visitors view or click the ads.

Hyperlink is a link from a hypertext file or document to another location or file, typically activated by clicking on a highlighted word or image on the screen.

Black Hat

In search engine optimization (SEO) terminology, black hat SEO refers to the use of aggressive SEO strategies, techniques and tactics that focus only on search engines and not a human audience, and usually does not obey search engines guidelines.

YouTube Video Marketing Overview

Getting Started

You get started by opening up a YouTube account. Go to www.YouTube.com and follow the step by step instructions. Then you open up a AdSense account. The AdSense account will take about a week to open. AdSense is linked to your YouTube account and land bank account. AdSense will use your 9 digit routing number to deposit a small amount of money into your land bank account. You then have to report to AdSense the amount deposited. After the deposit is confirmed, AdSense will send you a postcard to verify your address. You must then report to AdSense the pin number locate on the postcard. Once all the verification takes place YouTube allows you to connect all of the accounts and by doing so, you can now monetize your video's and create a passive income stream.

Social Media

You should join Social Media web sites like Facebook, Google Plus, Digg, Twitter, Linkedin, Tumbler and Pinterest. Every time you upload a video. When you are finished Optimizing it, you should link it to all of your social media web sites. This creates Backlinks. A Backlink is an incoming hyperlink from one webpage to another. Google and YouTube will rank your video higher if it has a good number of Backlinks. However if you have too many, and it appears that you have created them artificially, then Google and YouTube can punish you by removing your video.

YouTube Video Marketing Overview

As long as you are backlinking organically and not using Black Hat software or Black Hat web sites, you should be find with Google and YouTube.

Show Me the Money!

Monetization involves you allowing AdSense to place ads that run before or are placed on your videos. If the ads are clicked on, you make money. If the ads are viewed in their entirety you make money.

After you have your accounts set up, you need to gather all of the tools you will be using to create videos. You can create your videos using a standard video camera and tripod and videotape yourself. Or any other number of ways you can capture video. However for this program we are going "zero cost" s there will be no need to purchase or obtain a video camera.

Getting Free Tools to Create Your Videos

We are going to use "Screen Capture" software. Go to http://screencast-o-matic.com/home to download a free screen capture software called Screencast-o-Matic. There are two versions. The Free version allows you to videotape up to 15 minutes of content and places a watermark on all of your recordings. The pro version makes longer recordings and has edit tools and not watermark. The pro version cost $15 and year and may be worth the investment once your business begins to make a profit.

YouTube Video Marketing Overview

Then next tool you will use in creating your videos is a free copy of the office software package called Apache OpenOffice. Go to https://www.openoffice.org/download/ to download the software.

100% Copyright Free Content

Now that you have to tools to create a video, you need content. Wikipedia is an excellent source of copyright free content, you can use to create your videos. There are many keyword phrases that you can use to find material. Later on in this book you will learn how to use the Google Ad Planner to get the best keyword phrases to use in your videos.

YouTube Video Marketing
SEO – The Key to Internet Riches

Search Engine Optimization

Analytics: Video Viewership

Through out this book I am going to discuss many YouTube analytics that factor into how your video is ranked in YouTube. Once someone clicks onto your video to view it, YouTube keeps track of how many minutes it was view. Videos that are viewed from beginning to end get ranked higher base on the belie that the content is good if the viewer keeps watching it. For this reason, it is usually a good idea to keep most your videos under five minutes. It addition, this allows you to create more videos to a related topic. I is better to have twenty 3 minute videos than one 1 hour video, because it is more likely that the 3 minute videos will be watched in their entirety. Also by creating 20 videos you now have 20 possible places for AdSense to place monetized ads and thus increase your earning potential 20 times.

Tags, Keywords and Keyword Phrases

Tags, keywords and keyword phrases are the most important part of getting your YouTube video to rank on the first page of YouTube. There is an old saying..."If you commit murder, where do you hide the body, where nobody will find it? On the second page of Google".

YouTube Video Marketing
SEO – The Key to Internet Riches

Although we are working on YouTube the principle is the same. You must rank on the first page of YouTube in order for your video to get views from standard YouTube web site traffic.

Keywords are words that relate to your video. Some keywords for business are:

Business, Marketing and Start-up

Keyword Phrases for business are:

how to make money from home, internet marketing, small business grants

Tags are Keywords or Keyword Phrases that you place on your YouTube video's editing page, in order to get viewers to find your video.

Your goal is to try to rank in the top 20(land on the first page of YouTube) for every or most of the Tags in your video.

Your Video Title

The title of your video should be a keyword phrase that you want to rank for. It should also be relevant to the content in the video. When your title, tags and description are all relevant it boosts your YouTube rankings.

YouTube Video Marketing
SEO – The Key to Internet Riches

Video Description

Each video is allowed to have a description. At the top of the description box, is where you should place a clickable or hyperlink, to either your web site or another video that you wish to viewer to see. Below the link should be a description of the video that contains content that is relative to the video. One short cut you can use it to cut and paste your video script into the description.

You video description should also have the keywords you used as tags. This adds to the videos relevancy.

You should also put links in you video to your social media addresses.

Half Time Adjustments

Any tags that are ranking your video in the top 20 should be placed in the headline/title of the video to boost their rank even higher.

One software that helps save you a tremendous amount of time doing this is called Tube Buddy.

https://www.tubebuddy.com/

YouTube Video Marketing
Writing Your Script

CREATING CONTENT

You have two options for creating content. On screen video of yourself using a digital camera or phone camera. Take notes of what you will discuss.

Know your topic before you hit record.

Recording Tips:

* Use good lighting.

* Try recording near a window during the day time.

* Limit background noise as much as possible.

* Use a POWERPOINT screen capture style video.

* Create bullet points

* Use free software like jing or camstudio to record it. You can also get a free 30 day trial of camtasia from TechSmith

* www.screencast-o-matic.com is another free solution.

* Use your computer's built in microphone.

YouTube Video Marketing
Writing Your Script

* Use a usb microphone is ideal, but not required.

* if you or kids have a usb gaming headset that works as well.

* most smart phones have a mp3 recording option.

Writing Your Script

Try to use words in your script that get and hold you viewers attention. Words like... you, want, now, free limited time, All-American, imagine and how to, are just a few of the many words that are proven to stir a viewers emotions. Viewing a few copy writing videos on YouTube should help you to chose attentio grabbing words.

AIDA is an acronym used in marketing and advertising that describes a common list of events that may occur when a consumer engages with an advertisement.

- A – attention (awareness): attract the attention of the customer.
- I – interest of the customer.
- D – desire: convince customers that they want and desire the product or service and tha it will satisfy their needs.
- A – action: lead customers towards taking action and/or purchasing.

YouTube Video Marketing
Writing Your Script

Using a system like this gives one a general understanding of how to target a market effectively. Moving from step to step, one loses some percent of prospects.

AIDA is a historical model, rather than representing current thinking in the methods of advertising effectiveness.

A basic rule of thumb for writing your script is that one paragraph equals about 60 seconds of talking. So if you are trying to shoot a 3 minute video you what to create a 3 paragraph document for your script. Try to use words in our script that are relevant to the title of your video.

You can also cut and paste your script into a YouTube video editor, and make your video Closed Captioned. This will increase your rankings in the YouTube search engine and it will allow more people to understand your video and increase your views.

CREATING TOPICS FOR YOUR VIDEOS

It is time to brainstorm and write down topics for your videos.

Remember you could choose a video around your own information product if you had it.

YouTube Video Marketing
Writing Your Script

Get a notepad and think of 10 to 20 FAQ about your business.

http://answers.yahoo.com

Is a good source to find out what the potiential customers of your business are interested in.

Also look at articles on ezinearticles.com and see what topics come up the most for articles related to your business.

You can also browse forums related to your business

Take a look at information products about your target market.

When you make a video that features Frequently Asked Questions each faq could be a short 1 to 3 minute video.

Use nichesuggest.com for a list of possible keyword ideas as well as seocentro and the google keyword planner.

Brainstorm 5 to 10 additional solution oriented videos. You should cover why the solution you are offering is better and why does your product recommendation solve your customer's problem.

YouTube Video Marketing
Writing Your Script

Try to think of every advantage possible. Read other reviews of similar products or businesses or view sales pages for ideas of content for your videos.

Creating a Multipurpose Close

There are certain things that you should say in almost all of your videos:

* Thank the viewer for watching

* Ask the viewer to Thumbs up or Like your video

* Ask the viewer to subscribe to your YouTube Channel

* Ask the viewer to leave a comment

* Ask the viewer to share your video link with friends or social media

YOUR CALL TO ACTION

send your website visitors to a variety of places.

* A free website through weebly.com

* A free page through squidoo.com

* A free blog through blogspot.com

Use a tracking link like www.bit.ly or www.tinyurl.com

be careful as these links can change on you.

YouTube Video Marketing
Writing Your Script

UPLOADING VIDEO

Create your account at www.youtube.com you can use a google account if you have one already created. Upload your video. Then provide your keyword rich video title. Look at other examples of videos performing well in that space. Use keywords from your niche or business and topic research write a good description with the keywords in it.

Try to include at least 2 sentences in your description. More content in your description will not hurt you. Include your website link at the beginning of the description use format http://www.yourfreelink.com encourage likes, comments, or honest feedback at the end of the description. Make a call to action in the description as well.

Chapter 6

Best Way

To Write A

Business Plan

How to Write a Business Plan

Millions of people want to know what is the secret to making money. Most have come to the conclusion that it is to start a business. So how do you start a business? The first thing you do to start a business is to create a business plan.

A business plan is a formal statement of a set of business goals, the reasons they are believed attainable, and the plan for reaching those goals. It may also contain background information about the organization or team attempting to reach those goals.

A professional business plan consists of eight parts.

1. Executive Summary

The executive summary is a very important part of your business plan. Many consider it the most important because this part of your plan gives a summary of the current state of your business, where you want to take it and why the business plan you have made will be a success. When requesting funds to start your business, the executive summary is a chance to get the attention of a possible investor

2. Company Description

The company description part of your business plan gives a high level review of the different aspects of your business. This is like putting your elevator pitch into a brief summary that can help readers and possible investors quickly grasp the goal of your business and what will make it stand out, or what unique need it will fill.

3. Market Analysis

The market analysis part of your business plan should go into detail about your industries market and monetary potential. You should demonstrate detailed research with logical strategies for market penetration. Will you use low prices or high quality to penetrate the market?

4. Organization and Management

The Organization and Management section follows the Market Analysis. This part of the business plan will have your companies organizational structure, the type of business structure of incorporation, the ownership, management team and the qualifications of everyone holding these positions including the board of directors if necessary.

5. Service or Product Line

The Service or Product Line part of your business plan gives you a chance to describe your service or product. Focus on the benefits to the customers mor than what the product or service does. For example, a air conditioner makes cold air. The benefit of the product is it cools down and makes customers more comfortable whether they are driving in bumper to bumper traffic or are sick and sitting in a nursing home. Air Conditioners fill a need that could mean the difference between life and death. Use this section to state what are the most important benefit of your product or service and what need it fills.

6. Marketing and Sales

Having a proven marketing plan is a essential element to the success of any business. Today online sales are dominating the marketplace. Present a strong internet marketing plan as well as social media plan. YouTube videos, Facebook Ads and Press Releases all can be part of your internet marketing plan. Passing out flyers and business cards are still an effective way to reach potential customers.

Use this part of your business plan to state your projected sales and how you came to that number. Do your research on similar companies for possible statistics on sales numbers.

7. Funding Request

When you write your Funding Request section of your business plan, be sure to be detailed and have documentation of the cost of supplies, building space, transportation, overhead and promotion of your business.

8. Financial Projections

The following is a list of the important financial statements to include in your business plan packet.

Historical Financial Data

Your historical financial data would be bank statements, balance sheets and possible collateral for your loan.

Prospective Financial Data

The prospective financial data section of your business plan should show your potential growth within your industry, projecting out for at least the next five years.

You can have monthly or quarterly projections for the first year. Then project from year to year.

Include a ratio and trend analysis for all of your financial statements. Use colorful graphs to explain positive trends, as part of the financial projections section of your business plan.

How to Write a Business Plan

Appendix

The appendix should not be part of the main body of your business plan. It should only be provided on a need to know basis. Your business plan may be seen by a lot of people and you don't want certain information available to everybody. Lenders may need such information so you should have an appendix ready just in case.

The appendix would include:

Credit history (personal & business)

Resumes of key managers

Product pictures

Letters of reference

Details of market studies

Relevant magazine articles or book references

Licenses, permits or patents

Legal documents

Copies of leases

Building permits

Contracts

List of business consultants, including attorney and accountant

Keep a record of who you allow to see your business plan.

Include a Private Placement Disclaimer. A Private Placement Disclaimer is a private placement memorandum (PPM) is a document focused mainly on the possible downsides of an investment.

Chapter 7
Business
Insurance

BUSINESS INSURANCE

Consult an attorney for any and all of your business matters.

In the early 1990's an elderly woman purchased a hot cup of coffee from a McDonald's drive-thru window in Albuquerque. She spilled the coffee, and suffered 3rd degree burns. She sued Mcdonald's and won. She won 2.7 million dollars in a punitive damages victory. The verdict was appealed and settlement is estimated at somewhere in the neighborhood of $500,000 dollars. All because she spilled the coffee into her lap, while trying to add sugar and cream.

Two men in Ohio, were carpet layers. They were severely burned when a three and a half gallon container of carpet adhesive ignited, when the hot water heater it was sitting next to, was turned on. They felt the warning lable on the back of the can was insufficient. So they filed a lawsuit against the adhesive manufacturers and were awarded nine million dollars.

A woman in Oklahoma, purchased a brand new Winnebago. While driving it home, she set the cruise control to 70 miles per hour. She then left the drivers seat to make some coffee or a sandwich in the back of the motor home.

BUSINESS INSURANCE

The vehicle crashed and the woman sued Winnebago for not advising her, that cruise control does not drive and steer the vehicle. She won 1.7 million dollars and the company had to rewrite their instruction manual.

Unfortunately all three outrageous lawsuits are real. If you are going to run a business, any business, you should consider protecting yourself with Professional Liability Insurance, also known as Errors and Omissions (E & 0) insurance.

This type of insurance can help to protect you from having to pay the full cost of defending yourself against a negligence lawsuit claim.

Error and Omissions can protect you against claims that are not usually covered in regular liability insurance. Those policies usually cover bodily harm, or damage to property. Error and Omissions can protect you agaist negligence, and other mental anguish like inaccurate advice, or misrepresentation. Criminal prosecution is not covered.

Errors and Ommision insurance is recommended for notaries public, real estate brokers or investors and professionals like: software engineers, lawyers, home inspectors web site delvelopers and landscape architects to name a few professions.

BUSINESS INSURANCE

The Most Common Errors and Omission Claims:

%25 Breach of Fiduciary Duty

%15 Breach of Contract

%14 Negligence

%13 Failure to Supervise

%11 Unsuitability

%10 Other

BUSINESS INSURANCE

Things you should know about or require before purchasing a Errors and Omission policy is...

* What is the limit of liability

* What is the Deductible

* Does it include FDD First Dollar Defense - which obligates the insurance company to fight a case without a deductible first.

* Do I have Tail-end coverage or Extended Reporting Coverage (insurance that lasts into retirement)

* Extended coverage for Employees

* Cyber Liability Coverage

* Department of Labor Fiduciary Coverage

* Insolvency Coverage

If you get Errors and Omission insurance, renew it the day it expires. You must be careful to avoid gaps in your coverage, or it could result in not getting your policy renewed.

BUSINESS INSURANCE

A few E & O Insurance Providers:

Insureon

Insureon states that their median Errors and Omissions Insurance policy cost about $750 a year c about $65 a month. The price of course will vary according to your business, the policy you choose and other risk factors.

https://www.insureon.com/home

EOforless

EOforless.com helps insurance, investment, and real estate professionals buy E & O insurance at an affordable cost in five minutes or less.

https://www.eoforless.com/

BUSINESS INSURANCE

CalSurance Associates

As a leading insurance broker, CalSurance Associates, a division of Brown & Brown Program Insurance Services, Inc. has over fifty years of experience delivering comprehensive insurance products, exceptional service, and proven results to over 150,000 insured. They provide professionals nationwide and across multiple industries, including some of the largest financial firms and insurance companies in the United States.

http://www.calsurance.com/csweb/index.aspx

Better Safe Than Sorry

Insurance is one of the hidden costs of doing business. These are just a few companies and a brief overview on the topic of business insurance. Make sure to talk to an attorney or quailified insurance agent before making any decision on insurance. Protect you and your business. Many states do not require E & O insurances. But when you see the cost of some of the settlements, it's better to be safe than sorry.

Chapter 8

Business Terms

Business Terms & Definitions

Accounts – Companies produce a annual set of accounts. If you are listed on the stock exchange you have to give info on profits six months into the financial year.

Actuary – Actuaries work for insurance companies and pension providers and calculate life expectancy, accident rates and likely payouts by using math algorithms.

Business Plan – A business plan is a formal statement of business goals, reasons they are attainable, and plans for reaching them. It may also contain background information about the organization or team attempting to reach those goals.

Balance Sheet – a statement of the assets, liabilities, and capital of a business or other organization at a particular point in time, detailing, the balance of income and expenditure over the preceding period.

Business Terms & Definitions

Bear Market – A stock market in which share prices fall precipitously, typically 15%-20%.

Bull Market – A market when prices roar ahead.

Capital Gains – A capital gain refers to profit that results from a sale of a capital asset, such as stock, bond or real estate, where the sale price exceeds the purchase price. The gain is the difference between a higher selling price and a lower purchase price.

Capital Gains Tax – a tax levied on profit from the sale of property or of an investment.

Chapter 11 Bankruptcy – Chapter 11 is a chapter of Title 11 of the United States Bankruptcy Code, which permits reorganization under the bankruptcy laws of the United States. Chapter 11 bankruptcy is available to every business, whether organized as a corporation, partnership or sole proprietorship, and to individuals, although it is most prominently used by corporate entities.

Consumers Prices Index – The Consumer Price Index (CPI) is a measure that examines the weighte average of prices of a basket of consumer goods and services, such as transportation, food and medical care. It is calculated by taking price changes for each item in the predetermined basket of goods and averaging them.

Day Trading - Day Trading is the buying and selling of stocks during the trading day buy punters on their own account. The aim is to make a profit on the day and have no open positions at the close of the trading session.

Dow Jones Industrial Average – The Dow Jones Industrial Average (DJIA) is a price-weighted averag of 30 significant stocks traded on the New York Stock Exchange (NYSE) and the NASDAQ. The DJIA was invented by Charles Dow back in 1896.

Diminishing Returns – used to refer to a point at which the level of profits or benefits gained is less than the amount of money or energy invested.

Business Terms & Definitions

Economic Growth – Economic growth is the increase in the inflation adjusted market value of the goods and services produced by an economy over time. It is conventionally measured as the percent rate of increase in real gross domestic product or real GDP.

Equity – the value of the shares issued by a company.

Elasticity – elasticity is a measure of a variable's sensitivity to a change in another variable. In business and economics, elasticity refers the degree to which individuals, consumers or producers change their demand or the amount supplied in response to price or income changes.

Fiscal Year – The US fiscal year runs from October 1 to September 30.

Foreign Exchange (Forex) – Foreign exchange, or forex, markets are where one currency is exchanged for another.

Business Terms & Definitions

FORM 501 – A 501(c) organization is a nonprofit organization in the federal law of the United States according to 26 U.S.C. 501 and is one of 29 types of nonprofit organizations which are exempt from some federal income taxes.

Form 701 – General Information. Registration of a Limited Liability Partnership.

Grant – Grants are non-repayable funds or products disbursed or gifted by one party (grant makers), often a government department, corporation, foundation or trusts to a recipient, often (but not always) a nonprofit entity, educational institution, business or an individual.

Gross Domestic Product – GDP is the sum of all goods and services produced in the economy, including the service sector, manufacturing, construction, energy, agriculture and government.

Gross National Product – the total value of goods produced and services provided by a country during one year, equal to the gross domestic product plus the net income from foreign investments.

Hedge Funds – a limited partnership of investors that uses high risk methods, such as investing with borrowed money, in hopes of realizing large capital gains.

Income Statement – An income statement is one of the financial statements of a company and shows the company's revenues and expenses during a particular period.

Income Tax – tax levied by a government directly on income, especially an annual tax on personal income.

Inheritance Tax – a tax imposed on someone who inherits property or money.

Inflation – a general increase in prices and fall in the purchasing value of money.

Limited Liability Company (LLC) – A limited liability company (LLC) is a corporate structure whereby the members of the company cannot be held personally liable for the company's debts or liabilities. Limited liability companies are essentially hybrid entities that partnership or sole proprietorship.

Loan to Value – The loan-to-value (LTV) ratio is a financial term used by lenders to express the ratio o a loan to the value of an asset purchased. The term is commonly used by banks and building societies to represent the ration of the first mortgage line as a percentage of the total appraised value of real property.

Microloan – a small sum of money lent at low interest to a new business.

Business Terms & Definitions

Mutual Fund – an investment program funded by shareholders that trades in diversified holdings and is professionally managed.

NASDAQ – The National Association of Securities Dealers Automated Quotations (NASDAQ) was set up in 1971 as an international screen-based trading system without a central dealing floor. In 1998 it merged with the American Stock exchange (Amex).

Occupational Pension Scheme – Occupational pension schemes may be contributory or non-contributory, funded or unfunded, defined benefit or defined contribution. In contributory schemes, both you and your employer pay contributions towards the scheme. In non-contributory schemes, you do not contribute buy your employer does.

Partnership – A legal form of business operation between tow or more individuals who share management and profits. The federal government recognizes several types of partnerships. The two most common are general and limited partnerships. A limited partnership has both general and limited partners.

Rate of Return – A rate of return is the gain or loss on an investment over a specified time period, expressed as a percentage of the investment's cost. Gains on investments are defined as income received plus any capital gains realized on the sale of the investment.

Real Estate Investment Trusts – A real estate investment trust (REIT) is a company that owns, and in most cases operates, income-producing real estate. REITs own many types of commercial real estate, ranging from office and apartment buildings to warehouses, shopping centers and hotels.

SBA - The Small Business Administration (SBA0 is a U.S. Government agency, formulated in 1953, that operates autonomously. This agency was established to bolster and promote the economy in general by providing assistance to small businesses.

SCORE (SBA) – SCORE is a nonprofit organization that provides free business mentoring services to prospective and established small business owners in the United States. More than 10,000 volunteers provide these services, with all volunteers being active and retired business executives and entrepreneurs.

Sole Proprietorship – A business that legally has no separate existence from its owner. Income and losses are taxed on the individual's personal income tax return. The sole proprietorship is the simplest business form under which one can operate a business. The sole proprietorship is not a legal entity.

Tax Haven – Generic term for geographical area outside the jurisdiction of one's home country which imposes only a few restriction on legitimate business activities within its jurisdiction, and little or no income tax. Also called a low tax jurisdiction, non tax jurisdiction, or offshore haven.

Business Terms & Definitions

Value Added Tax – A value added tax (VAT) is a consumption tax added to a product's sales price. It represents a tax on the "value added" to the product throughout its production process.

Wall Street – Wall Street is a street in lower Manhattan that is the original home of the New York Stock Exchange and the historic headquarters of the largest U.S. Brokerages and investment banks.

Yield – The yield is the income return on an investment, such as the interest or dividends received from holding a particular security. The yield is usually expressed as an annual percentage rate based on the investment's cost, current market value or face value.

Zero Interest Rates – A zero interest rate policy is a route taken by a central bank to keep the base rate at zero percent in an attempt to stimulate demand in the economy by making the supply of money cheaper.

$10,000

Massive Money Internet Marketing &

Copy Writing & SEO Course &

$1,000 Value Bonus

Internet Marketing Videos

LIBRARY I (Video Training Programs)

1. Product Creation
2. Copy Writing & Payment
3. Auto Responder & Product Download Page
4. How to start a Freelancing business
5. Video Marketing
6. List Building
7. Affiliate Marketing
8. How to Get Massive Web Site Traffic

LIBRARY II (Video Training Programs)

1. Goldmine Government Grants
2. How to Write a Business Plan
3. Secrets to making money on eBay
4. Credit Repair
5. Goal Setting
6. Asset Protection How to Incorporate

$10,000 MegaSized Internet Marketing &

Copy Writing & SEO Course &

$1,000 Value Bonus

Library III

1. SEO SIMPLIFIED PART 1

2. SEO SIMPLIFIED PART 2

3. SEO Private Network Blogs

4. SEO Social Signals

5. SEO Profits

Bonus 1000 Package!

1. Insider Secrets to Government Contracts (PDF)

2. 1000 Books/Guides (text files)

3. Vacation Discounts (text file w/links to discounts)

4. Media Players (3 Software Programs)

100% MONEY BACK GUARANTEE!!!

ALL ON A 8 GIGABYTE FLASH DRIVE

This Massive Library with a $10,000 value all for only a

1 time payment **of $67!!!**

Get Instant Access by Using the Link Below:

https://urlzs.com/p7v3T

Leave a review and join Our VIP Mailing List Then Get All our Audio Books Free! We will be releasing over 100 money making audio books within the next 12 months! Just leave a review and join our mailing list and get them all for free!

Just Hit/Type in the Link Below

https://urlzs.com/HfbGF

9 781951 929145